50 uplifting funny stories

for seniors

*"Golden Laughter: 50 Uplifting and
Funny Tales for Seniors"*

Table of content

Introduction

"50 Uplifting funny Stories for Seniors" is a heartwarming collection designed to provide comfort, joy, and inspiration to older individuals. Each story serves as a gentle reminder of the beauty in everyday moments, the resilience of the human spirit, and the value of a life well-lived. These tales touch upon themes of love, friendship, family, and the wisdom that comes with age, offering a source of positivity and connection for seniors as they navigate their unique journeys. Whether shared during quiet moments or within the company of loved ones, these stories aim to uplift and bring smiles to the faces of those who have lived rich and meaningful lives.

The Secret Garden Revisited

In a quiet neighborhood, nestled behind an old house, there lay a forgotten corner of land. Once a vibrant garden, it had fallen into disrepair over the years, its beauty hidden beneath layers of neglect. But fate had something special in store for this forgotten sanctuary.

Ella, a spirited senior with a heart full of memories and a longing for purpose, gazed out at the neglected space from her kitchen window. Her eyes sparkled with a mix of nostalgia and determination. One sunny morning, armed with a pair of gardening gloves and a heart full of hope, Ella ventured into the overgrown wilderness.

With each pull of a weed, each gentle touch of a flower, Ella felt a renewed sense of energy. She pruned, she planted, and she lovingly nurtured the soil back to life. Weeks turned into months, and as the seasons danced, the secret garden began to awaken.

One day, as Ella stepped into the garden, she noticed a fragile, colorful butterfly fluttering about. It danced among the blossoms, as if whispering tales of far-off lands. Ella smiled, realizing that her garden had become a haven not only for plants but for the creatures that sought its beauty.

Word spread through the neighborhood about Ella's secret garden. Curious neighbors and friends came to visit, their faces lighting up with awe as they stepped through the garden gate. Some brought their grandchildren, who delighted in the magic of this hidden paradise.

Ella's garden became a source of inspiration and connection. Seniors from the nearby retirement home joined her in planting, watering, and sharing stories of their own. Laughter and companionship filled the air, and the garden blossomed not only with flowers but with the bonds of newfound friendships.

As Ella sat on a weathered bench in her secret garden one sunny afternoon, she marveled at the transformation that had taken place. The once-forgotten corner was now a vibrant tapestry of colors and scents, a living testament to the power of love and dedication.

With a contented sigh, Ella whispered to herself, "Life has its seasons, just like a garden. And even when things seem forgotten, there's always a chance for beauty to bloom again." And as the sun dipped below the horizon, casting a warm golden glow on the garden, Ella's heart overflowed with gratitude for the journey that had led her to rediscover the magic of the secret garden.

The Pen Pal Adventure

Once upon a time in the cozy corners of a senior community, a group of adventurous retirees decided to embark on a unique journey – The Pen Pal Adventure. With pens in hand and a mischievous glint in their eyes, they began corresponding with pen pals from around the world.

One day, Mildred, an 80-year-old retiree, received a letter from her pen pal, Pablo, who lived in Spain. He described the vibrant festivals and lively dances that filled his town's streets. Inspired by his words, Mildred gathered her friends and announced, "We're going to have our own fiesta right here!"

As the seniors set their plans in motion, they faced comical challenges. Harold attempted to flamenco dance and ended up in a tangle of limbs, causing everyone to burst into laughter. Mildred, determined to make authentic paella, accidentally mistook a spice for paprika and created the spiciest dish anyone had ever tasted.

Undeterred by their mishaps, the group of seniors threw their fiesta. They decorated the community hall with colorful streamers and played Spanish music that made their feet tap and hips sway. With their unique version of the flamenco dance, they giggled their way through a memorable performance that had everyone clapping along.

Word of the seniors' hilarious fiesta spread, and soon they received letters of admiration and amusement from their pen pals. The Pen Pal Adventure had not only connected them with friends from afar but had also brought joy, laughter, and a little spice to their lives.

And so, in that senior community, friendships blossomed, hearts were warmed, and the Pen Pal Adventure became a legendary tale that was passed down to inspire future generations of adventurous souls.

Second Chance at Love

In the charming town of Willowbrook, two elderly neighbors, Edith and George, found themselves navigating the winding path of a second chance at love. Both had lost their spouses many years ago, and their lives had settled into routines of solitude.

One sunny morning, fate intervened when a mischievous squirrel knocked over Edith's bird feeder, sending seeds raining onto George's porch below. Annoyed at first, Edith hobbled downstairs to retrieve her feeder and found George trying to shoo away the squirrel with a broom. Their eyes met, and laughter erupted as they realized the absurdity of the situation.

From that moment on, their lives intertwined in a series of endearing mishaps. Edith accidentally watered George's flowers, thinking they were her own, and George mistook Edith's cat for a burglar one night, leading to a flurry of apologies and chuckles. As they shared stories over cups of tea and plates of cookies, their hearts began to mend, and a deep connection blossomed.

One day, George decided to take a bold step. He invited Edith to the town's annual dance, an event neither had attended in years. With a twinkle in her eye, Edith accepted, and they embarked on a quest to find the perfect dance outfits. Their shopping escapades turned into a comical parade of mismatched outfits and outrageous hats, leaving them both in stitches.

When the night of the dance arrived, Edith and George stepped onto the dance floor with a mix of nervousness and excitement. As they swayed to the music, their feet occasionally tripping over each other, the room seemed to fade away, leaving only the warmth of their laughter and the joy of being together.

Their second chance at love became an inspiration to the entire town, reminding everyone that it's never too late to find happiness and companionship. Edith and George's story proved that life's greatest adventures can begin in the most unexpected and delightful ways, and that love, even in the later years, is a journey worth taking.

The Grandparents' Day Out

It was Grandparents' Day, and the senior residents of Harmony Hills Retirement Home were buzzing with excitement. The staff had planned a special day out for them, and they were all eager to embark on their adventure.

As the group gathered in the lobby, a cheerful bus driver named Betty introduced herself. "Alright, everyone, buckle up for our Grandparents' Day Out!" she announced with a grin. With the seniors settled in their seats, the bus set off, and the journey began.

Their first stop was a local zoo, where the seniors marveled at the exotic animals. However, the highlight was when a mischievous monkey managed to snatch a pair of glasses right off Harold's face. The seniors erupted in laughter as Harold tried to negotiate with the monkey for their safe return.

Next, they visited an amusement park. Mildred, a sprightly 85-year-old, decided to conquer her fear of heights and bravely joined the line for the roller coaster. As the ride roared to life, Mildred's shrieks of terror turned into delighted laughter, and she emerged from the ride with a triumphant smile.

Lunchtime brought another hilarious twist. The group stopped at a quaint diner, and Mildred and George decided to share a massive banana split. As they dug in, whipped cream and chocolate sauce ended up everywhere except in their mouths. Their sticky faces and laughter-filled attempts to clean up provided entertainment for the entire restaurant.

The day concluded with a relaxing boat ride on a tranquil lake. As the seniors drifted along, they shared stories of their own childhood adventures and dreams. The sun set in a spectacular display of colors, casting a warm glow over the group as they basked in the beauty of the moment.

Back at Harmony Hills, the seniors returned with hearts full of joy and memories that would last a lifetime. Their Grandparents' Day Out had been a day of laughter, camaraderie, and unexpected escapades. The seniors realized that age was just a number, and that the spirit of adventure could thrive at any stage of life. As they bid farewell to Betty the bus driver, they knew that this was a day they would cherish and talk about for years to come.

The Legacy Quilt

In the heart of Maplewood Manor, a group of spirited seniors embarked on a heartwarming journey called "The Legacy Quilt." Determined to leave a lasting mark, they decided to create a quilt that would tell the story of their lives, one square at a time.

The seniors gathered in the common room, armed with fabric swatches, needles, and a healthy dose of enthusiasm. The first challenge arose when they realized that none of them quite remembered how to sew. After a series of comical attempts at threading needles and mismatched stitches, they dubbed themselves "The Quilted Quandary."

Undeterred by their lack of sewing finesse, they decided to turn their mishaps into a patchwork of humor. Each square of the quilt became a canvas for their creativity and shared memories. Agnes stitched a square depicting her daring skydiving adventure at age 75, while Henry embroidered a scene from his bungled attempt at baking a cake that ended up resembling a science experiment.

Mildred's square was a tribute to her lifelong love of dancing, featuring a pair of meticulously sewn ballet slippers – despite the fact that Mildred had two left feet in real life. And Harold contributed a square showcasing his infamous garden mishaps, including the time he planted carrots and ended up growing turnips instead.

As the quilt took shape, so did the bond between the seniors. They shared stories, laughter, and a sense of camaraderie that filled the room with warmth. Even the staff members joined in, offering their sewing expertise and adding their own patches to the quilt.

One evening, they gathered around the quilt, which was now a riotous tapestry of memories and laughter. They marveled at the quirky squares, reminiscing about their shared experiences and the joy they had found in the process. And when the time came to unveil the quilt to the rest of the residents, the room was filled with awe and admiration.

The Legacy Quilt became a cherished centerpiece at Maplewood Manor, a symbol of the seniors' resilience, humor, and the beautiful mosaic of their lives. It was a testament to the power of shared creativity and a reminder that even in the later years, new friendships and unforgettable memories could be woven together with laughter and love.

Lost and Found Memories

In the cozy corners of Silver Haven Retirement Home, a group of spirited seniors embarked on a unique journey called "Lost and Found Memories." Armed with determination and a touch of mischief, they set out to rediscover forgotten moments from their past.

One sunny afternoon, Mildred stumbled upon an old, dusty trunk in the attic. The trunk was filled with an eclectic mix of items – faded photographs, handwritten letters, and even a pair of retro disco shoes. As the seniors gathered around, Mildred exclaimed, "Let's use these items to relive our favorite memories!"

Their first challenge was deciphering the handwritten letters, which turned out to be love notes exchanged between two residents, Agnes and Henry, decades ago. The seniors decided to reenact their sweet love story, complete with exaggerated accents and blushing faces. Agnes and Henry laughed until tears streamed down their cheeks, as their love story came to life once more.

The disco shoes sparked a lively dance-off, with Harold and Mildred attempting to recreate the iconic moves from their younger days. Their hilarious dance routines had everyone in stitches, and even the staff joined in, creating a whirlwind of laughter and nostalgia.

As they browsed through the old photographs, they stumbled upon an image of Edith posing with a vintage car. Edith's eyes twinkled as she recounted her days as a daring drag racer in her youth. Inspired by her story, the seniors transformed their courtyard into a makeshift racetrack, complete with cardboard cars. The races were a riot, with walkers and canes serving as imaginary steering wheels.

Their adventure reached its peak when they found a forgotten recipe book. The seniors decided to host a cooking competition, attempting to recreate dishes from their past. Hilarity ensued as they navigated the kitchen, resulting in dishes that ranged from mildly edible to downright disastrous. Despite the mishaps, their culinary creations were a testament to the joy of shared experiences.

As the day drew to a close, the seniors gathered around a campfire in the courtyard, under a starlit sky. They shared stories, sang songs, and reveled in the magic of the memories they had rediscovered. In those moments, they realized that lost memories could be found again, not only in forgotten items but in the bonds of friendship and the laughter of shared adventures.

And so, the "Lost and Found Memories" became a cherished tradition at Silver Haven, a reminder that no memory is truly lost if it's treasured in the hearts of those who share it.

Musical Connections

In the heart of Harmony Meadows Senior Center, a group of spirited seniors embarked on a tuneful adventure known as "Musical Connections." With instruments in hand and a touch of whimsy, they set out to prove that age was just a number when it came to making music.

Their journey began when the seniors decided to form a band – aptly named "The Silver Serenaders." Henry, an energetic 90-year-old, took up the drums, despite his family's initial shock. "I've always wanted to be the heartbeat of a band!" he declared with a mischievous grin.

Mildred, with her delicate fingers, chose the piano. However, her enthusiasm sometimes led to unexpected chord changes that transformed a classic ballad into a jazzy romp. The resulting melodies had everyone tapping their feet and giggling.

Agnes, with her velvet voice, became the lead vocalist. Her renditions of old favorites left not a dry eye in the room, even though her memory sometimes led her to forget a verse or two. And then there was Edith, who turned her walking cane into a makeshift conductor's baton, leading the group with gusto.

One sunny afternoon, as they practiced their repertoire, a curious thing happened. The strains of music drew a local school's marching band to their doorstep. The youngsters, wide-eyed and curious, joined the seniors in a joyous jam session that transcended generations. The brass instruments mingled with the piano, the drums kept a steady rhythm, and Agnes' voice soared in perfect harmony with the young voices.

The result was a symphony of laughter and shared moments that resonated far beyond the walls of Harmony Meadows. The unexpected collaboration became a source of inspiration for the seniors and a heartwarming example of how music could bridge the gap between ages.

As word of their musical connections spread, the Silver Serenades found themselves invited to perform at local events, spreading joy and laughter wherever they went. Their performances were characterized by charming imperfections and a genuine spirit that touched the hearts of all who listened.

"Musical Connections" had not only created a band but had woven a tapestry of laughter, friendship, and shared passion for music. The seniors learned that age was no barrier to forming new connections and that the power of music could transform even the simplest moments into something extraordinary.

The Art of Friendship

In the heartwarming realm of Sunny Pines Retirement Village, a group of lively seniors decided to embark on a whimsical quest known as "The Art of Friendship." With paintbrushes and a colorful imagination, they set out to create a masterpiece that would celebrate their bond in the most creative way.

Gathered around a table laden with paints, canvases, and an assortment of brushes, the seniors quickly realized that their artistic skills varied greatly. Agnes, a former art teacher, wielded her brush with finesse, creating intricate scenes of nature and landscapes. Meanwhile, Harold, whose attempts at stick figures often puzzled his grandchildren, boldly declared, "I'll paint with my heart!"

As they dipped their brushes into vibrant colors and painted side by side, laughter filled the room. Mildred playfully splashed paint on George's canvas, leading to a playful paint fight that left them all covered in an abstract array of colors. Henry, known for his fondness for puns, exclaimed, "We're making a real 'work' of art!"

The masterpiece began to take shape, reflecting the unique personalities of each artist. Agnes' serene scenes blended harmoniously with Harold's bold and vibrant strokes. Edith added her whimsical touch by incorporating a few cat-shaped clouds, inspired by her beloved feline companion.

However, the real twist came when they decided to create a collaborative section where each senior would paint on another's canvas. The result was a delightful mishmash of styles that perfectly mirrored the tapestry of their friendship.

With the finishing touches applied, they proudly unveiled their creation to the rest of the retirement village. The room was filled with gasps of amazement and peals of laughter as they explained the story behind each stroke of the brush. The residents couldn't help but be captivated by the beauty of their united efforts and the joy that radiated from the canvas.

"The Art of Friendship" became a cherished symbol at Sunny Pines, a reminder that friendship is a masterpiece that's best created with laughter, shared experiences, and a colorful spirit. The seniors' collaborative creation not only adorned the walls but also warmed the hearts of all who admired it, a testament to the enduring bond that age couldn't diminish and creativity only enhanced.

Unexpected Adventures

In the tranquil town of Willowbrook, a group of adventurous seniors at the Silver Lining Retirement Home found themselves swept up in a series of unexpected adventures that would leave them chuckling for years to come.

It all began with a game of bingo that took an unexpected turn. Mildred, known for her enthusiasm, shouted "Bingo!" a little too excitedly, causing her chair to tip backward and her to topple onto the floor. The room erupted in laughter as Mildred emerged, slightly disheveled but with an undiminished spirit, holding her winning bingo card triumphantly.

Inspired by the laughter, the seniors decided to embrace the spirit of spontaneity and embark on a series of "Random Acts of Fun." One sunny morning, they surprised the local parkgoers by staging an impromptu dance-off. Their wobbly yet exuberant moves drew a crowd, and soon, strangers joined in the dance, creating a merry spectacle.

Their adventures didn't stop there. One afternoon, they organized a "Picnic of Surprises" in their courtyard. Each senior contributed a unique dish, resulting in a delightful mishmash of flavors and textures that had everyone guessing what they were eating. Henry's "mystery meatballs" turned out to be veggie-filled delights, while Edith's "secret salad" was a concoction of unexpected ingredients that had everyone in stitches.

Their most memorable escapade, however, Involved a treasure hunt that led them on a wild goose chase around the retirement home. Clues were hidden in the most unexpected places – from the bottom of the fish tank to the garden gnome's hat. Agnes, the puzzle master, had devised a complex trail that left the seniors scratching their heads and doubled over in laughter.

After a day filled with treasure hunt shenanigans, the seniors gathered around a bonfire in their courtyard. They shared stories of their unexpected adventures, reminiscing about the laughter, surprises, and newfound friendships that had blossomed from their willingness to embrace the unexpected.

Their unexpected adventures became a cherished tradition at Silver Lining Retirement Home, a testament to the fact that life's most delightful moments often arise when you least expect them. The seniors learned that a little spontaneity, a dash of humor, and a sprinkle of camaraderie could turn even the simplest activities into unforgettable escapades that would warm their hearts for years to come.

The Generous Gardener

In the heart of Whispering Meadows Senior Community, a sprightly senior named George had earned the endearing title of "The Generous Gardener." Armed with his trusty watering can and a knack for growing the most vibrant blooms, George's garden had become the talk of the town.

One sunny morning, Mildred, a fellow resident, approached George with a twinkle in her eye. "George, I heard your roses have a secret," she said, a mischievous grin playing on her lips.

George chuckled, his eyes crinkling with amusement. "Secret? Well, Mildred, my roses do have a secret ingredient."

Mildred leaned in, intrigued. "Do tell, George."

George leaned closer and whispered, "It's all in the music. I play my favorite tunes to them every day."

Mildred burst into laughter, envisioning George serenading his roses with a garden hose as a makeshift microphone. "You're telling me your roses are jamming to music?"

George nodded, a playful glint in his eyes. "Absolutely! They respond to different genres. Classical for the elegant roses, jazz for the sassy ones, and even a bit of rock 'n' roll for the rebellious ones."

Mildred couldn't help but imagine the scene – George tending to his garden, dancing along with his plants as they swayed to the music. She playfully suggested, "Well, George, maybe you should have a concert for your roses."

George's eyes lit up, and the idea took root. That weekend, George invited the entire senior community to his garden for a "Concert for the Roses." As they gathered around, George donned an exaggerated conductor's hat, and with a flourish, he raised his watering can, mimicking a conductor's baton.

With a playlist that ranged from Beethoven to Elvis, George guided his fellow seniors in a lighthearted performance that had everyone laughing and swaying along. Mildred, holding a sunflower like a microphone, belted out a "serenade" to her favorite flower, sending peals of laughter through the crowd.

As the sun set and the concert came to an end, George surveyed his garden, now illuminated by twinkling fairy lights. He smiled, a contented glint in his eyes, knowing that he had not only nurtured beautiful blooms but also cultivated a garden of joy and shared laughter.

"The Generous Gardener" became a beloved figure in Whispering Meadows, a reminder that a touch of humor and a bit of music could transform even the simplest activities into moments of pure delight. And as the seniors left George's garden that evening, they carried with them the memory of a laughter-filled concert that had bloomed from the generosity of a gardener's heart.

The Dance of Memories

In the heartwarming halls of Golden Years Senior Center, an annual event called "The Dance of Memories" was the highlight of the year. The seniors eagerly anticipated the night when they would dust off their dancing shoes and waltz down memory lane.

Edith, known for her impeccable sense of style, decided to take the lead this year. She donned a dazzling sequined gown and a pair of dancing shoes that sparkled almost as much as her eyes. "Get ready for the dance of a lifetime!" she announced with a twirl.

As the music began, the seniors took to the dance floor, their movements a delightful blend of grace and laughter. Agnes and Henry shared a twirl that turned into a giggle-filled spin, while Mildred and George attempted a cha-cha that resembled a spirited shuffle.

However, the true star of the evening was Harold, who had been secretly practicing a surprise dance routine. When the time came, he took center stage, wearing a pair of oversized sunglasses and a wide grin. As the upbeat music played, Harold transformed into a disco sensation, grooving to the beat with the energy of a teenager.

The crowd erupted into applause and laughter as Harold spun and shuffled, his dance moves a delightful combination of old-school disco and hilarious improvisation. Mildred even threw in a few dance moves of her own, creating a duet that had everyone in stitches.

As the dance came to an end, the seniors exchanged smiles and stories of the memories they had relived through their joyful dance. They realized that the "Dance of Memories" wasn't just about the steps; it was about the moments shared, the laughter echoed, and the friendships celebrated.

And so, each year, the seniors of Golden Years Senior Center continued to dance, not just through the steps of the waltz or the twirls of the cha-cha, but through the tapestry of memories they had woven together. "The Dance of Memories" became a cherished tradition, a reminder that no matter the age, dancing through life with laughter and camaraderie could create the most beautiful and uplifting memories of all.

The Baking Club

In the heart of Serenity Oaks Retirement Community, a group of spirited seniors formed a baking club that quickly became the talk of the town. With flour on their aprons and a dash of mischief in their eyes, they embarked on a series of baking adventures that would leave everyone with a sweet tooth and a belly full of laughter.

Their club meetings turned into delightful chaos as Mildred, known for her mischievous sense of humor, accidentally mistook salt for sugar in her cookie recipe. The resulting "salty surprise" cookies had everyone grimacing and giggling, but they couldn't help but marvel at Mildred's ability to turn a baking mishap into a hilarious memory.

Not to be outdone, George, the resident "pie enthusiast," attempted a complex lattice pattern on his apple pie. However, his artistic skills took a detour, resulting in a pie that looked more like a playful game of tic-tac-toe. Despite its unconventional appearance, George's pie quickly disappeared as the seniors indulged in a slice of his good-natured creativity.

Agnes, the baking club's unofficial leader, introduced a "mystery ingredient challenge." Each member had to incorporate a surprise ingredient into their dish. When the day of reckoning arrived, they discovered that Edith had added a touch of hot sauce to her blueberry muffins. The combination of sweet and spicy had everyone reaching for water and wiping away tears of laughter.

One day, the club decided to host a bake sale to raise funds for a local charity. The senior bakers took their mission seriously, donning aprons and chef's hats with an air of determination. But as they meticulously arranged their goods on the tables, chaos ensued when Mildred's dog, Max, decided to join the festivities and ended up snagging a scone.

The seniors couldn't help but dissolve into laughter as Max happily pranced around with his prize, and Mildred playfully scolded him for his "culinary critique." The bake sale turned into a delightful mix of sweet treats and furry escapades, with Max becoming the unofficial mascot of the baking club.

"The Baking Club" at Serenity Oaks Retirement Community became more than just a place to whip up delicious treats; it became a haven of laughter, friendship, and the joy of shared experiences. The seniors' culinary creations may have been sprinkled with a touch of chaos, but their bonds were as warm and comforting as a freshly baked batch of cookies.

Rediscovered Talent

In the cozy corner of Maplewood Senior Center, a group of seniors were on a mission to "Rediscover Talent." As they shared stories of their past, they realized that hidden talents and passions were waiting to resurface.

One day, Agnes mentioned her forgotten love for playing the harmonica. The group eagerly encouraged her to give it a try, and as she blew into the harmonica, a soulful melody filled the room. The seniors were stunned by Agnes's skill and urged her to perform at the upcoming talent show.

As the talent show approached, Mildred revealed that she had once been a master of balloon animals. With determination, she grabbed a bag of balloons and started twisting. The room quickly filled with colorful animals, and laughter followed as Mildred's creations seemed to take on a life of their own.

George, the quiet painter of the group, discovered his hidden talent for storytelling. He shared tales of his youth, sprinkled with imaginative twists that had everyone captivated. His storytelling was so enthralling that they decided to turn it into a regular "Story time with George" event.

On the night of the talent show, Agnes took the stage with her harmonica, filling the room with a bluesy melody that touched everyone's hearts. Mildred followed, showcasing her balloon animal menagerie with comedic flair, leaving the audience in stitches.

Finally, George stepped up, sharing a whimsical tale of an adventurous squirrel that had the crowd laughing and cheering for more. The seniors realized that their talents had not only entertained but also connected them in a way that felt like rediscovering old friends.

As the applause filled the room, the seniors beamed with pride. "Rediscovered Talent" had not only uncovered hidden abilities but also reignited their zest for life and created a tapestry of laughter and camaraderie. It was a reminder that age couldn't dim the brilliance of their talents, and that sometimes, all it took was a little encouragement and a lot of laughter to reveal the treasures within.

The Wisdom Circle

In the heart of Harmony Haven Retirement Home, a group of wise and whimsical seniors formed "The Wisdom Circle." With cups of tea in hand and twinkle-eyed determination, they gathered to share life's insights in the most unexpected and amusing ways.

One day, as they sat beneath a sun-dappled tree, Mildred posed a philosophical question, "If you could go back in time, what advice would you give your younger self?"

Henry, the resident jokester, leaned forward with a mischievous smile. "I'd tell myself to invest in banana peels – they'll be the next big thing!"

Laughter echoed through the circle, and soon, their "time-travel advice" took a hilariously absurd turn. Agnes suggested learning to speak squirrel for better backyard conversations, and George advocated for mastering the art of interpretive dance to communicate with pets.

Their laughter didn't just echo in the courtyard; it became the cornerstone of The Wisdom Circle. They realized that wisdom wasn't always about serious advice – it was also about finding joy in the little moments and sharing laughter with friends.

One afternoon, Edith brought her ukulele, and their Wisdom Circle evolved into a spontaneous sing-along. They belted out classic tunes with gusto, substituting lyrics with their own comical versions. Passersby couldn't help but smile at the sight of the "Serenading Sages," proving that music and laughter held timeless wisdom of their own.

The Wisdom Circle wasn't just about sage advice; It was a haven of humor, camaraderie, and the delightful realization that life's best lessons were often wrapped in laughter. As the sun set on another gathering, the seniors realized that they were not only sharing their wisdom but also nurturing friendships that would shine as brightly as the stars in the night sky.

A Gift of Time

In the heart of Serene Haven Retirement Home, a delightful senior named Martha found herself facing an unexpected challenge. With her eyesight not as sharp as it used to be, she often mixed up her daily routines, leading to a series of comical escapades.

One sunny morning, Martha decided to tackle a puzzle in the common room. However, her "puzzle pieces" turned out to be a stack of napkins, much to her confusion. Chuckling, the other residents joined in, helping her unravel the mystery while creating a new type of puzzle – "The Napkin Conundrum."

The laughter continued as Martha embarked on a "culinary adventure." Confusing salt for sugar and cinnamon for pepper, she managed to concoct a dish that left everyone's taste buds in shock. Yet, her infectious laughter turned the mishap into a cherished memory, leading the residents to affectionately refer to her cooking as "Martha's Mystery Meals."

As the days passed, the residents began to see the gift that Martha's unique perspective brought to their community. Her "mix-ups" became a source of joy and a reminder that time was a precious gift to be cherished.

Inspired by Martha's spirit, the residents decided to host an event called "A Gift of Time." They set up a clock-themed gathering, complete with time-themed games, treats, and decorations. Martha was the guest of honor, and she embraced her role as the "Time Keeper" with gusto.

During the event, Martha shared her favorite stories and life lessons, weaving her mix-ups into tales of laughter and wisdom. The room was filled with joy and camaraderie, a testament to the idea that life's most memorable moments often sprouted from unexpected twists.

As the event came to a close, Martha thanked everyone for the gift of their time and laughter. The "Gift of Time" had not only celebrated Martha's unique perspective but had also emphasized the importance of embracing each moment, no matter how unpredictable it might be.

And so, in the heart of Serene Haven, Martha's "mix-ups" became a treasured reminder that life's most valuable gifts weren't always wrapped in perfection, but in the shared laughter and connections that made every moment unforgettable.

The Travel Diaries

In the charming community of Evergreen Meadows Retirement Village, a group of adventurous seniors came together to form "The Travel Diaries." Armed with maps, magnifying glasses, and a touch of wanderlust, they set out on a series of delightful escapades without ever leaving their beloved village.

Their first adventure took them to "Paris" – a meticulously decorated room with Eiffel Tower cutouts and croissants on every table. Agnes, always the drama enthusiast, put on a beret and declared herself the "Tour Guide Extraordinaire." As she spoke in a heavy French accent, the seniors couldn't help but laugh, feeling as though they had been magically transported to the City of Light.

For their "African Safari," they transformed the courtyard into a wildlife haven. Henry, armed with a binoculars and a stuffed lion, led the group on a hilarious "safari tour" that included sightings of "exotic" creatures like squirrels and garden gnomes. Laughter echoed as they "spotted" a rare "pink flamingo" in the community pond – actually just a neighbor's inflatable pool toy.

The Travel Diaries' most memorable expedition was their "Space Odyssey." With cardboard rocket ships and an impressive collection of aluminum foil helmets, they boldly went where no senior had gone before. As they "orbited" the courtyard, Edith's trusty walking cane accidentally knocked over a potted plant, leading to a flurry of giggles and "zero-gravity gardening."

Their adventures weren't confined to their village – they even held a "Cruise Ship Spectacular" in the common room, complete with deck chairs, ocean sounds, and Mildred's attempt at a hula dance that had everyone rolling with laughter.

The Travel Diaries became more than just themed gatherings; they were a testament to the seniors' unwavering spirit, creativity, and the joy of shared experiences. Through their lighthearted escapades, they discovered that the greatest journeys didn't always require a passport – sometimes, all it took was a bit of imagination and a lot of laughter to create memories that would last a lifetime.

The Book Club Chronicles

In the cozy corner of Oakwood Senior Center, a group of spirited seniors formed "The Book Club Chronicles." Their passion for reading was only rivaled by their knack for turning literary discussions into uproarious adventures.

At one meeting, they delved into a classic mystery novel that had them all on the edge of their seats. However, as they debated possible suspects and motives, George, known for his absentmindedness, accidentally revealed the ending. The room erupted in laughter, and Mildred quipped, "Well, that's one way to solve a mystery!"

Embracing the unexpected, they decided to give their book club gatherings unique twists. They dressed as characters from their chosen books, turning into a colorful array of literary figures from Sherlock Holmes to Jane Eyre. Agnes, dressed as a mischievous wizard, even attempted to cast a "spelling bee" spell on her fellow members, leading to a chorus of laughter and amusing word mix-ups.

For their themed meeting on romance novels, they turned the room into a "Love Café," complete with heart-shaped decorations and a menu of fictional food from their favorite stories. As they discussed romantic plots, George, a self-proclaimed baker, surprised them with a cake that was decorated with a frosting rendition of Romeo and Juliet – who appeared to be wearing mismatched socks!

Their book club gatherings became legendary in the senior center, with their whimsical approach to literary discussions drawing both laughter and inspiration. And so, "The Book Club Chronicles" became a tale of shared laughter, imaginative twists, and the realization that even the pages of a book could be a gateway to delightful adventures that spanned beyond the written word.

The Community Garden

In the heart of Blossom Grove Retirement Community, a group of green-thumbed seniors decided to cultivate their own oasis of laughter and camaraderie with "The Community Garden."

One sunny day, Mildred excitedly announced her grand plan to introduce exotic plants to the garden. She proudly presented her "tropical" selection – including a cactus, a palm tree, and even a rubber plant. The group burst into laughter, envisioning their community garden transformed into a desert oasis.

Not to be outdone, George, a retired botanist, decided to experiment with a hybrid vegetable. He meticulously crossed a tomato with a bell pepper and proudly unveiled his creation – a "toma-pepper" that left everyone chuckling at the audaciousness of his horticultural innovation.

The garden soon became a place of friendly competition, with each senior tending to their own corner of paradise. Agnes declared herself the "Garden Guardian," armed with a watering can and a wide-brimmed hat that was more suitable for a safari than a garden. Her enthusiastic patrols and dramatic exclamations had the garden buzzing with laughter.

One day, the group decided to host a "Garden Fashion Show," where they adorned their plants with hats, scarves, and even sunglasses. As they paraded their decked-out flora, the garden transformed into a whimsical runway that had everyone in stitches.

Their garden produce may not have "been the most conventional, and their gardening techniques often raised eyebrows, but the bonds they formed and the laughter they shared were a testament to the beauty of their community. The Community Garden wasn't just a place to grow plants; it was a space where seeds of friendship were sown, nurtured, and blossomed into a colorful tapestry of shared joy and lighthearted moments.

From Fear to Freedom

In the "From Fear to Freedom" workshop for seniors, a charming mix-up occurred during a group activity. The facilitator had intended to demonstrate overcoming fear by having participants do a trust fall exercise. However, due to a hilarious miscommunication, when the facilitator called out "Ready, set, go!" instead of falling backward, all the seniors enthusiastically leaped forward into a group hug, creating a spontaneous and heartwarming embrace. Laughter filled the room as they realized the delightful mix-up, and the facilitator joined in on the laughter too. The activity turned into a beautiful symbol of the supportive and uplifting environment the workshop aimed to create, leaving everyone with a sense of freedom from their fears and a memory of that joyous moment.

The Laughing Yoga Club

At "The Laughing Yoga Club" for seniors, a mischievous squirrel somehow found its way into the tranquil garden where the class was being held. As the seniors engaged in their laughter-filled yoga routine, the squirrel decided to play along. It hopped onto one of the mats and began mimicking the participants, contorting its tiny body in amusing ways. The seniors couldn't contain their laughter at this unexpected furry addition to the class. With each stretch and pose, the squirrel seemed to be teaching its own version of "squirrel yoga." The sight of the seniors and the squirrel sharing a laughter-infused yoga session became the talk of the town, bringing smiles to everyone who heard the heartwarming tale.

The Reunion Surprise

At "The Reunion Surprise" event for seniors, a retiree named Martha decided to take matters into her own hands. She secretly organized a surprise flash mob performance with her fellow attendees. As the reunion went on, a lively oldies song began to play, and suddenly Martha and a group of seniors burst into a choreographed dance routine that they had been practicing in secret. The surprised looks on their friends' faces quickly turned into smiles and laughter as they joined in on the impromptu dance party. Even the event organizers were taken aback, but they quickly embraced the unexpected turn of events. The dance floor transformed into a scene of pure joy and camaraderie, proving that age is just a number and that reunions can be full of delightful surprises that make cherished memories.

The Memory Lane Marathon

During "The Memory Lane Marathon" for seniors, a heartwarming and unexpected connection unfolded between two participants, John and Mary. As they were sharing stories from their past, they realized they had both attended the same dance event many decades ago but had never met back then. To recreate that special moment, they decided to have a spontaneous dance-off right there in the middle of the event. Their lively moves and infectious laughter drew a crowd, and soon enough, other participants joined in, dancing to tunes from their era. The dance floor became a nostalgic haven where seniors relived their youthful energy and created new memories together, proving that the bonds formed on Memory Lane are timeless and can lead to joyful moments even later in life.

Another uplifting tale from "The Memory Lane Marathon" involves a group of seniors who decided to share their favorite childhood hobbies. As they gathered around, each participant demonstrated their unique skills, from yo-yo tricks to kite flying. One participant, Harold, showcased his impressive collection of vintage model trains. As he set up the tracks and the trains started chugging along, the room was filled with awe and childlike wonder. Other seniors soon joined him, helping set up a miniature world of nostalgia and sparking conversations about their own childhood hobbies. The event transformed into a delightful showcase of talents and passions, reminding everyone that no matter their age, the things that brought them joy in the past can still light up their lives today.

Artistic Expressions

In another heartwarming tale from "Artistic Expressions," a group of seniors collaborated on a large mural that depicted scenes from their lives and shared memories. Each participant contributed their unique artistic style, resulting in a mosaic of colors, shapes, and stories that told a beautiful tale of their shared experiences. As they worked side by side, the participants bonded over their art, exchanged life stories, and formed connections that went beyond the canvas. The completed mural became a cherished symbol of their unity and the transformative power of art in fostering meaningful connections among seniors.

The Seniorpreneurs

This story features a group of retired friends who collaborated to launch a unique walking tour business in their town. Drawing from their deep knowledge of the area's history and culture, they designed captivating tours that took participants on a journey through time. Their storytelling skills and camaraderie turned each tour into an engaging experience, attracting both locals and tourists alike. Through their entrepreneurial venture, these seniors not only generated income but also showcased the rich heritage of their community while enjoying each other's company and making lasting memories.

The Wisdom of Nature

In "The Wisdom of Nature" retreat for seniors, a group of individuals gathered amidst the serene beauty of a forest. Led by a naturalist guide, they embarked on a journey to connect with the natural world and discover the lessons it had to offer. One day, as they sat by a tranquil stream, they observed a caterpillar undergoing its transformative journey into a butterfly.

The guide shared the metaphorical significance of this process: how life's changes, much like the caterpillar's metamorphosis, could lead to beautiful transformations. Inspired by this lesson, the seniors decided to each write down a personal challenge they were facing and tie it to a tree branch. Over the course of the retreat, they revisited the tree, witnessing their challenges transform into colorful paper butterflies, symbolizing their growth and resilience.

As the retreat came to an end, the seniors found themselves not only rejuvenated by their time in nature but also deeply connected to each other and the profound wisdom that the natural world had imparted. They left the retreat with a renewed sense of hope and a reminder that, just like the butterfly emerging from its cocoon, they too could embrace change and experience beautiful transformations in their lives.

The Knitting Circle

In "The Knitting Circle" for seniors, a delightful mix-up occurred when two participants, Martha and Harold, accidentally swapped their knitting projects. Martha had been working on a cozy blanket while Harold had been diligently crafting a scarf. When they realized their mistake, instead of unraveling the yarn, they decided to have some fun with it.

Martha and Harold continued knitting each other's projects, resulting in a whimsical combination of a blanket with scarf-like fringes. As they worked side by side, the other members of the knitting circle couldn't help but chuckle at the unexpected creation taking shape before their eyes. The colorful mishmash of stitches became a symbol of friendship, laughter, and the joy of embracing mistakes.

When the blanket-scarf hybrid was finally complete, Martha and Harold decided to auction it off during a charity event. The unique creation quickly became a hit, and its quirky backstory captured the hearts of the attendees. The auction turned into a lively affair filled with laughter and friendly bidding wars, and the blanket-scarf ended up raising more funds for charity than anyone had anticipated.

The Knitting Circle members fondly remembered the "fusion project" as a testament to their creativity, camaraderie, and the wonderful moments of laughter that brightened their weekly gatherings.

The Language Exchange

At the local senior center, a group of enthusiastic seniors decided to participate in a "Language Exchange" program where they would learn new languages from each other. One day, Margaret, who was known for her witty sense of humor, stood up and said, "I've been trying to learn Spanish, but every time I say something, my dog gives me a funny look. I think I accidentally taught him Spanish instead!"

The group erupted in laughter, and from that day on, their language exchange sessions became a delightful mix of language learning and hilarious anecdotes about talking pets and lost-in-translation mishaps.

The Legacy Letters

A group of seniors decided to write their own legacy letters as a fun project. As they gathered to share their letters, one gentleman stood up and said, "In my letter, I told my grandkids all about the wisdom I've gained over the years. I advised them to always put money in the freezer... because everyone knows that's the coolest place in the house!"

The room burst Into laughter as everyone shared their own quirky pieces of advice, creating a light-hearted and memorable experience for all.

The Senior Athletes

In a small town, a group of spirited seniors formed their own sports team called "The Senior Striders." They decided to enter a local relay race, and their enthusiasm was infectious. On race day, as they lined up with the other teams, their opponents couldn't help but chuckle at the sight of these determined seniors.

When the race started, the Senior Striders took off with surprising speed, but their coordination was a bit questionable. At one point, George mistook a water station volunteer for a teammate and handed him the baton, prompting laughter from the crowd. Meanwhile, Susan, a retired gymnast, attempted a cartwheel as she passed the baton, creating a comical diversion.

Despite their unconventional techniques, The Senior Striders reached the finish line with beaming smiles and a contagious spirit. They may not have won the race, but they certainly won the hearts of everyone present with their joyful energy and undeniable camaraderie.

The Healing Power of Music

At the senior community center, a music therapist named Emily held weekly sessions where she played soothing tunes for the residents. One day, Emily decided to switch things up and introduced a karaoke machine to add some fun to the session. The seniors were intrigued but a bit hesitant at first.

As the karaoke began, something magical happened. Mildred, a retired librarian known for her quiet demeanor, picked up the microphone and belted out a surprisingly powerful rendition of an old rock 'n' roll classic. The room was stunned into silence before erupting into cheers and applause.

Inspired by Mildred's unexpected performance, others took turns at the microphone. Harold, who usually relied on a walker, got up and did an energetic air guitar solo that had everyone in stitches. Even Emily, the music therapist, joined in with an amusing interpretive dance.

From then on, the healing power of music took on a whole new meaning at the center. Laughter became a regular part of the music therapy sessions, as the seniors discovered that letting loose and embracing their inner rock stars was a fantastic way to lift their spirits and bond with one another.

The Friendship Bench

At the senior center, there was a special bench known as "The Friendship Bench," where residents would gather to chat, share stories, and offer support to one another. One day, as a group of seniors sat on the bench, they noticed a mysterious package placed nearby with a note that read, "For the bravest soul."

Intrigued and amused, the seniors decided to open the package, revealing a collection of outrageous hats and wigs. The note inside read, "Put on your silliest hat and wear it proudly for a day of laughter and friendship!"

The seniors eagerly donned the wigs and hats, transforming themselves into a group of whimsical characters. Helen, usually the prim and proper lady of the group, sported a neon green wig that made her resemble a lively parrot. George, a retired firefighter, wore a towering top hat that seemed to defy gravity.

As they paraded around the senior center, they couldn't help but attract attention and laughter from fellow residents. Passersby joined in, and soon the entire center was filled with joyous laughter and camaraderie. Even the staff members got in on the fun, with the director of the center wearing a rainbow afro wig.

"The Friendship Bench" became a symbol of unity and lightheartedness, reminding everyone that laughter is a universal language that can bridge generations and bring people closer together. And so, the tradition of wearing silly hats on the bench continued, creating cherished memories and strengthening the bonds of friendship among the seniors.

The Technology Trailblazers

In a retirement community, a group of seniors decided to form "The Technology Trailblazers" club to conquer the world of modern gadgets. Armed with smartphones, tablets, and laptops, they embarked on a journey to unravel the mysteries of the digital age.

At their first meeting, there was a mix of excitement and uncertainty. Eleanor, a former schoolteacher, accidentally took a selfie while trying to answer a call, causing everyone to burst into laughter. As they fumbled with touchscreens and buttons, their determination shone through.

Over the weeks, they navigated through tech tutorials and troubleshooting, often with hilarious results. Jim, a retired engineer, mistook the voice command feature for a magic genie, exclaiming, "Play some Frank Sinatra, my friend!" much to everyone's amusement.

Their journey led to unexpected friendships and shared moments of triumph and hilarity. One day, they managed to set up a video call with a grandchild living abroad, only to find they were showing off their noses more than anything else.

Through their perseverance and a healthy dose of humor, "The Technology Trailblazers" not only embraced modern technology but also found a new source of joy and connection. They proved that you're never too old to learn and that laughter truly is the best app for the soul.

The Poetry Circle

In a cozy corner of the senior center, a group of seniors gathered for their weekly Poetry Circle. Edna, known for her knack for rhyming, took the lead and announced, "Today, let's write poems about our favorite desserts!"

As they shared their verses, the room filled with laughter and creative energy. Harold, a retired plumber, penned a poem that went, "Oh, chocolate cake, you make my heart ache, but it's a sweet pain I'll gladly take!" His dramatic recitation had everyone in stitches.

Not to be outdone, Mildred contributed her own quirky haiku: "Ice cream so cold, my taste buds are sold, brain freeze, I'm told!" The group erupted in laughter, recognizing the all-too-familiar sensation.

But the highlight of the session was when Walter, a retired teacher, stood up and recited a heartfelt ode to a donut that he claimed had "changed his life." He passionately described the glazed delicacy as if it were a long-lost love, earning him a standing ovation from his fellow poets.

Their poems, while humorous, also carried a sense of nostalgia and shared memories. The Poetry Circle became a space where they not only explored their creativity but also found joy in connecting over the simple pleasures of life. And so, each week, they continued to craft verses that were equal parts amusing and heartwarming, creating a tapestry of laughter and camaraderie.

The Intergenerational Cooking Class

At the local community center, an intergenerational cooking class was organized, pairing tech-savvy teenagers with spirited seniors to share culinary skills. Martha, an 80-year-old with a passion for baking, was paired with Jake, a 17-year-old aspiring chef armed with a smartphone.

As they embarked on their cooking adventure, Martha was amazed by the array of gadgets and apps Jake used. When he introduced her to a food delivery app, she exclaimed, "Back in my day, we had to actually go to the store! No wonder I never learned to text; I was too busy walking for groceries!"

The real hilarity began when they attempted a complicated recipe that involved multitasking and precise measurements. As Martha fumbled with the smartphone to follow the recipe, she accidentally dialed her grandson, who ended up on a three-way video call, watching the cooking chaos unfold.

Amid the chaos, they managed to whip up a mishmash of ingredients that Jake optimistically dubbed "fusion cuisine." With laughter echoing in the kitchen, they tasted their creation, sharing hearty laughs over the unexpected flavors.

In the end, Martha and Jake didn't just create a memorable meal; they forged an unforgettable bond. The cooking class became a delightful blend of generations, where the wisdom of experience met the enthusiasm of youth, all seasoned with a generous sprinkle of laughter.

The Joy of Volunteering

At the local senior center, a group of retirees decided to embrace the joy of volunteering by organizing a "Helping Hands Brigade" to assist with various community events. Their enthusiasm was unmatched, but their first attempt didn't exactly go as planned.

For their debut project, they volunteered to help set up a charity bake sale at a local park. Armed with aprons, spatulas, and an abundance of good intentions, they arrived early in the morning to set up their booth. However, things quickly took a comical turn when Henry, a retired chef, accidentally spilled a bag of flour, turning himself into a "flour-covered ghost."

The laughter didn't stop there. Mildred, an avid gardener, mistook powdered sugar for actual sugar, resulting in an overly sweet batch of cookies that prompted surprised reactions from unsuspecting customers. Meanwhile, George, a former engineer, built an intricate display stand that had one minor flaw – it collapsed under the weight of a giant cupcake, leaving everyone in stitches.

Despite the mishaps, their infectious spirit and laughter drew a crowd, and soon people were lining up to buy their unique creations. Passersby were entertained by the brigade's good-natured banter and hilarious attempts at baking perfection.

While the bake sale might not have been a culinary triumph, it became a memorable and heartwarming display of the joy of volunteering. The seniors discovered that their willingness to laugh at themselves and embrace the unexpected brought a different kind of sweetness to the event – a reminder that the true joy of volunteering often lies in the camaraderie and shared moments of laughter with others.

The Legacy of Dance

At the senior center, a group of spirited retirees decided to showcase their love for dancing by hosting a "Legacy of Dance" performance. Each senior would present a dance style from their era, creating a lively and nostalgic event.

As the rehearsals began, it became clear that some of the dance moves from their youth had become a bit rusty. Mildred, a former ballerina, attempted a graceful pirouette but ended up doing a pirouette-salsa hybrid that had everyone in stitches. George, a retired disco enthusiast, attempted a signature move but got caught in his own sequined pants.

Yet, their determination and sense of humor were unwavering. During one practice, Henry, a jazz aficionado, accidentally tripped and fell into the arms of the tap-dancing group, turning their routine into an impromptu tango. The unexpected blend of dance styles had everyone in uproarious laughter.

On the night of the performance, the audience was treated to a delightful showcase of dance moves that spanned generations. As each senior took the stage, they danced their hearts out, showcasing their unique styles and creating a tapestry of laughter and joy.

The highlight of the evening was a grand finale where all the seniors joined in for a dance-off that seamlessly mixed waltz, hip-hop, and even a little breakdancing. The audience couldn't help but join in the laughter and applause, appreciating not just the dance moves but also the unbridled spirit and camaraderie of the seniors.

The "Legacy of Dance" performance became a celebration of life's rhythm and the enduring power of laughter, proving that no matter the age, the joy of dancing and sharing a good laugh is truly timeless.

The Humor Therapy

At the senior center, a new and unconventional program called "Humor Therapy" was introduced to boost the residents' spirits. The idea was simple: laughter is the best medicine. The participants gathered in a circle, ready to embark on a laughter-filled journey.

As the session began, the leader, a lively comedian named Max, shared a series of humorous anecdotes and jokes. He recounted a tale of a talking parrot that outsmarted a burglar, causing uproarious laughter among the seniors.

Then came the twist. Max instructed everyone to stand up and engage in a "laughter yoga" exercise. The room filled with hearty guffaws, belly laughs, and even some snorts. The initial self-consciousness gave way to genuine amusement, and soon, the seniors were laughing so hard that they couldn't catch their breath.

In the midst of the laughter chaos, Eleanor, a retired librarian with a penchant for witty one-liners, accidentally let out a snort that sounded like a trumpet. The room burst into even more laughter, and Eleanor playfully declared herself the "Snort Symphony Conductor."

The session continued with light-hearted improve games and playful interactions that had everyone in stitches. One round involved coming up with the silliest uses for a rubber chicken, resulting in creative and hilarious suggestions.

As the "Humor Therapy" session concluded, the seniors left with lighter hearts and a renewed sense of joy. They realized that laughter truly was a powerful form of therapy, and they had discovered a new way to connect with each other and embrace the lighter side of life.

And so, the senior center became a place where "Humor Therapy" sessions were eagerly anticipated, where laughter became a healing force, and where the Snort Symphony Conductor's legendary snorts brought smiles to all.

The Lifelong Learners

At the local community center, a group of spirited seniors proudly called themselves "The Lifelong Learners." They were known for their insatiable curiosity and their determination to learn new things, no matter their age.

One day, they decided to take up a challenging new skill: breakdancing. They enlisted the help of a patient and enthusiastic dance instructor named Alex, who was equal parts amazed and amused by their enthusiasm.

During their first lesson, the seniors found themselves attempting various breakdancing moves with varying degrees of success. Mildred, a retired schoolteacher, attempted a windmill spin but ended up spinning like a top, eliciting laughter from the group. George, a former banker, tried to do the worm but ended up looking more like a caterpillar in slow motion.

Despite the hilarious mishaps, their determination was unbreakable. They practiced tirelessly, often turning their dance sessions into laugh-filled social gatherings. Each failed spin and wobbly step only fueled their determination to master the art of breakdancing.

As the weeks went by, their progress was evident. They managed to pull off a synchronized routine that combined classic dance moves with their own unique twists. The routine had the perfect blend of graceful spins and joyful improvisations, and it left everyone in stitches.

When the day of their public performance arrived, "The Lifelong Learners" took the stage with confidence. As they danced, their passion and energy were infectious, and the audience couldn't help but cheer and applaud. The seniors finished their routine with a group pose that looked like a cross between a freeze and a yoga pose, and the crowd erupted into laughter and applause.

"The Lifelong Learners" had not only added breakdancing to their repertoire of skills but also created a lasting memory that highlighted their willingness to embrace the joy of learning and share laughter along the way. Their performance was a testament to the fact that age is just a number, and that the pursuit of knowledge and laughter knows no bounds.

The Outdoor Movie Nights

Every summer, the seniors at the community center eagerly anticipate their beloved "Outdoor Movie Nights." One warm evening, as the sun sets and the stars twinkle above, a delightful mix-up turns a regular movie night into a hilarious adventure.

As the projector beams to life, the movie's title appears on the screen: "The Grand Voyage." The crowd settles into their lawn chairs, ready to enjoy a heartwarming tale of exploration. However, as the movie starts, it becomes apparent that something has gone awry – the audio is in a language none of them understand!

Confusion quickly gives way to laughter as the seniors invent their own hilarious dialogue for the characters on screen. Mildred, known for her quick wit, playfully interprets the protagonist's dramatic lines with a comical twist. Walter, with his booming voice, creates a whole backstory for the quirky sidekick, causing uproarious laughter from the group.

Soon, others join in, voicing their interpretations and adding witty commentary. The movie's original plot takes a backseat as the seniors craft their own whimsical storyline filled with inside jokes and clever quips. The once-serious characters on screen become endearing caricatures of their real selves.

As the movie comes to a close, the seniors applaud their own impromptu performance and share stories of their favorite moments from their hilarious version of "The Grand Voyage." The mix-up becomes the talk of the town, and subsequent movie nights are eagerly anticipated for the unique, uproarious experience they bring.

"The Starlit Mix-Up" becomes a cherished memory in the history of "Outdoor Movie Nights." It serves as a reminder that the best moments are often the unplanned ones, filled with laughter, camaraderie, and the joy of creating new stories together under the twinkling stars.

The Senior Storytellers

In the cozy gathering space of "The Senior Storytellers," a mischievous twinkle lights up the eyes of Eleanor, the group's sprightly prankster. Eleanor hatches a plan to inject some excitement into their regular meetings.

At the next storytelling session, Eleanor weaves a hilarious tale about a daring bingo heist. The story follows a group of spirited seniors who, tired of the same old bingo routine, decide to spice things up. They devise an elaborate scheme to swap the bingo numbers with outrageous alternatives, leading to uproarious chaos during the game.

As Eleanor narrates, the room fills with laughter. Her fellow storytellers chime in with embellishments and anecdotes of their own, sharing their own humorous twists on the bingo caper. The room is alive with their infectious joy, and they can barely contain their laughter as they imagine seniors wearing feather boas and oversized sunglasses as they call out zany bingo numbers.

Inspired by Eleanor's story, the group decides to play a lighthearted round of bingo using their own creative set of numbers. The traditional game transforms into a riotous event, with seniors chuckling, teasing each other, and making playful remarks about the absurd number choices.

Eleanor's story becomes a legendary tale among "The Senior Storytellers," a reminder that even in their golden years, they can continue to create unforgettable memories and find joy in the simplest, most unexpected moments. And so, their gatherings are forever marked by the memory of "The Great Bingo Caper," a story that brought laughter, camaraderie, and a renewed sense of youthful mischief to their lives.

The Nature Walks Club

In the heart of a serene retirement community, a spirited group of seniors forms the "Nature Walks Club." Led by their fearless leader, Mr. Thompson, these nature enthusiasts embark on weekly expeditions to explore the beauty of the great outdoors. Little do they know, their escapades will soon become the stuff of legend.

On one sunny morning, the club sets out for a peaceful stroll through a nearby forest. As they admire the flora and fauna, they come across a picturesque pond with a charming little bridge. Excitement fills the air as they decide to cross the bridge for a closer look.

Just as the last member steps onto the bridge, it gives an ominous creak before collapsing into the pond below! Gasps turn into laughter as they realize everyone is safe, albeit a bit wet. The members of the Nature Walks Club share knowing glances and chuckles, dubbing the incident

Undeterred by their soggy mishap, the group presses on. Their adventure takes an unexpected turn when they encounter a mischievous squirrel who seems to be leading them deeper into the woods. They follow the squirrel's antics, imagining it as their furry tour guide, and dub it "Squirrelly Sam."

Later, during a snack break, they discover their picnic supplies have been swiped by a crafty raccoon. Instead of getting upset, they dub the raccoon "Ranger Rob" and share a good-natured laugh. Mr. Thompson turns to the group and says, "Looks like the wildlife wants to join our club too!"

With each outing, the Nature Walks Club faces new and amusing challenges. From mistaking a tree stump for a rare bird to getting caught in an impromptu rain dance, their misadventures bring them closer together and create lasting memories.

At the club's annual gathering, members recount their escapades with uproarious laughter. They celebrate not only the beauty of nature but also the joy of shared experiences and the friendships that have blossomed along the way. The Nature Walks Club becomes a symbol of resilience, humor, and the simple pleasures of life, reminding everyone that laughter truly is the best trail companion.

The Pen Pals Across Continents

In the cozy lounge of the senior center, a group of lively seniors excitedly gathers for their weekly Pen Pals Across Continents meeting. Each member has a pen pal from a different part of the world, and their exchanges have turned into a heartwarming, and often hilarious, global connection.

One day, Mildred, whose pen pal lives in Japan, shares a tale that has everyone in stitches. She recounts a mix-up with cultural references that led to an unintentionally amusing misunderstanding. Mildred had mentioned sending her "favorite snack, peanut butter and jelly sandwiches," assuming it was a universal treat. To her surprise, her pen pal was both puzzled and amused, as peanut butter and jelly isn't a common combination in Japan. Mildred's pen pal had replied, "I look forward to experiencing this curious sandwich phenomenon!"

The group erupts in laughter, and soon, they're all sharing their own comical cultural mix-ups. Henry, who corresponds with a pen pal in Australia, confesses that he once mentioned wearing his "favorite thongs" during a beach day. His pen pal had written back, equally puzzled, about how interesting it was that he enjoyed wearing flip-flops on his feet.

As the laughter subsides, the seniors reflect on the joy their pen pal connections have brought them. Each member shares anecdotes of not only the amusing misunderstandings but also the heartwarming moments of cultural exchange, friendship, and the realization that humor transcends borders.

The Pen Pals Across Continents group continues to meet, weaving a tapestry of laughter and connection that spans the globe. Their stories serve as a reminder that no matter the distance, age, or cultural differences, the universal language of humor and friendship can create bonds that brighten even the golden years of life.

The Legacy of Art

Once upon a time in the vibrant senior community of Willowwood, an unusual art class was about to begin. The instructor, Miss Agnes, was known for her quirky personality and passion for bringing out the hidden talents of her students.

One day, she introduced the concept of "Doodle Dilemmas" – a challenge where each senior had to create a piece of art around a random, silly scenario. The room filled with laughter as they drew a giraffe riding a unicycle in a rainstorm or a cow disco dancing under a disco ball.

As the weeks passed, Miss Agnes noticed something remarkable happening. Not only were the seniors creating whimsical masterpieces, but they were also forging new friendships and building an unexpected legacy. Their art was displayed all around Willowwood, and soon people from neighboring towns were coming to witness the "Doodle Dilemmas" exhibit.

One day, a renowned art critic arrived, expecting to see traditional works of art. Instead, he was greeted by an uproariously funny display of senior doodles. At first, he was baffled, but as he wandered through the exhibit, he found himself laughing uncontrollably and appreciating the sheer joy and creativity emanating from each piece.

The Legacy of Art was born – not as a stuffy collection of highbrow pieces, but as a celebration of the seniors' laughter, camaraderie, and newfound passion for doodling. Their legacy spread far and wide, reminding everyone that art is not just about technical skill, but about the joy it brings and the connections it fosters. And so, Willowwood became a place where age was just a number, and the legacy of art was a testament to the timeless spirit of creativity and community.

The Seniors' Wisdom Podcast

In the heart of the Sunshine Pines retirement community, a group of lively seniors decided to embark on a new adventure – they were starting their very own podcast called "The Seniors' Wisdom." Led by the spirited Miss Mildred, who had a knack for witty anecdotes and sage advice, the group aimed to share their life lessons in a lighthearted and entertaining way.

Their first episode, titled "The Great Laundry Mishap," recounted the hilarious tale of Mr. Johnson accidentally dyeing his white shirts pink and trying to convince everyone he was embracing a new fashion trend. As the seniors chuckled through the story, listeners were treated to a valuable lesson in embracing life's little mishaps with grace and humor.

In another episode, "Navigating Technology 101," the group delved into their comical encounters with modern gadgets. Miss Mildred's attempt to use a TV remote as a phone had everyone in stitches, but her subsequent advice on embracing technology without fear struck a chord with both seniors and tech-savvy youngsters.

As the podcast gained popularity, the Sunshine Pines seniors found themselves with a dedicated following, including not just their fellow residents, but also young listeners who cherished the timeless wisdom wrapped in laughter. Each episode became a testament to the fact that age is no barrier to learning, sharing, and connecting with others.

The pinnacle of their podcasting journey came when they invited a renowned comedian as a guest. The lively banter between the generations created an episode titled "Laughter Knows No Age," where the comedian marveled at the seniors' wit and humor while sharing his own stories of performing on stage. It was an episode that left everyone with tears of joy and a newfound appreciation for the intergenerational bond.

"The Seniors' Wisdom Podcast" became more than just a collection of stories; it became a symbol of the enduring spirit of the elderly – a reminder that age is just a number, and laughter is the universal language that brings people together across generations. And so, in the cozy corner of Sunshine Pines, the podcast continued to uplift, entertain, and spread wisdom, proving that life's golden years are meant to be celebrated with joy, laughter, and a touch of podcasting flair.

The Seniors' Flash Mob

In the charming town of Harmonyville, the local senior center was known for its lively and adventurous group of residents. One sunny afternoon, Miss Betty, an energetic and mischievous senior, had a brilliant idea: a surprise flash mob to bring joy to the town.

Miss Betty gathered her fellow seniors and whispered her plan – they would perform a spontaneous dance routine in the town square. The idea was met with laughter and excitement, and soon enough, the seniors began practicing their dance moves in secret.

On the chosen day, as the clock struck noon, the town square was bustling with people going about their business. Suddenly, a familiar tune started playing through hidden speakers, and out of nowhere, the senior flash mob burst into action. Miss Betty led the way with her energetic dance moves, and soon enough, the whole square was transformed into a vibrant dance party.

Passersby couldn't believe their eyes as seniors of all ages – some using canes, others twirling their walkers – grooved to the music with unmatched enthusiasm. Even the town's mayor couldn't resist joining in on the fun, showing off his surprisingly smooth dance skills.

The crowd erupted In cheers and applause, and even a few tears of joy were shed. As the dance routine came to an end, the seniors struck a final pose, basking in the well-deserved admiration from the townspeople. The event was captured on video and quickly went viral, spreading smiles far beyond Harmonyville.

The seniors' flash mob became an annual tradition, eagerly anticipated by both the residents and visitors to the town. Miss Betty and her crew continued to surprise everyone with their spirited dance routines, proving that age is no obstacle to spreading laughter and happiness.

And so, in the heart of Harmonyville, the seniors' flash mob became a symbol of the town's vibrant spirit and a testament to the fact that life's best moments are meant to be celebrated with a dance, a smile, and a touch of joyful spontaneity.

The Family Recipe Cookbook

In the cozy senior living community of Maplewood Meadows, a heartwarming project was brewing among a group of lively residents. Inspired by their shared love for good food and fond memories, they decided to create "The Family Recipe Cookbook."

The idea was simple: each senior would contribute their favorite family recipe along with a hilarious or heartwarming story that went along with it. Miss Edna kicked things off with her famous apple pie recipe, recounting the time she accidentally used salt instead of sugar, creating a pie that had her family laughing for days.

Mr. Henry, a retired fisherman, shared his secret fish chowder recipe that had been passed down through generations. He regaled the group with the tale of the time he caught an extra slippery fish that managed to escape three times before finally landing in his pot.

As more recipes poured in, so did the laughter and camaraderie. Miss Lillian's spaghetti sauce mishap, where she mistook chili powder for oregano, left everyone in stitches. And who could forget the uproarious tale of Mr. Jenkins attempting to recreate his grandmother's famous fried chicken, only to end up with a kitchen covered in flour and feathers?

The seniors' cookbook quickly became a cherished treasure, not just for its delicious recipes, but for the priceless stories that accompanied each dish. Families and visitors would often gather in the community lounge to hear these tales of culinary mishaps and triumphs.

The project culminated in a grand "Cook-Off and Storytelling" event, where the seniors prepared their signature dishes for a lively tasting party. As laughter echoed through the halls and the aroma of delicious food filled the air, it was clear that the cookbook had brought everyone together in a unique and heartwarming way.

"The Family Recipe Cookbook" became a testament to the power of shared experiences and the joy that comes from embracing both the successes and mishaps that make up a lifetime of cooking. In Maplewood Meadows, the cookbook not only filled the bellies of its residents but also nourished their spirits, reminding them that the best memories are often found in the simple pleasures of a good meal and hearty laughter.

The Generational Story Swap

In the cozy corner of the Sunrise Seniors Community Center, a remarkable event known as "The Generational Story Swap" was about to unfold. Every Friday, a group of spirited seniors gathered to share tales from their past, but today, they decided to add a delightful twist.

As the event kicked off, the room was buzzing with anticipation. Mildred, the sprightly 90-year-old, took the stage first. With a twinkle in her eye, she regaled the audience with a story about her wild adventures in the 1940s, dancing the jitterbug until dawn and getting chased by a mischievous goat during a country fair.

Next up was Alex, the charismatic 30-something grandson of one of the seniors. He recounted his daring escapade of attempting to learn salsa dancing for a friend's wedding, only to find himself with two left feet and tripping over his own shoelaces. The room erupted in laughter, and the seniors couldn't help but chuckle at the familiar feeling of youthful clumsiness.

The true magic of the story swap, however, came when Ethel, a wise 78-year-old, took the stage. She began to share her recent misadventures with modern technology, attempting to set up her new smartphone and accidentally sending emoji's to her grandchildren. The room was in stitches as they related to the struggles of adapting to a fast-paced digital world.

As the stories continued, the generations blended seamlessly. George, a retired pilot, shared tales of soaring through the skies in vintage airplanes, and Lily, a young nurse, recounted heartwarming stories of bringing comfort to patients during difficult times.

In the end, the Generational Story Swap was a heartwarming success. Laughter echoed through the room, and the seniors found common ground through shared experiences, both old and new. The event not only bridged the generation gap but also created lasting friendships and a sense of unity that transcended age.

And so, week after week, the seniors and their young counterparts continued to gather, each bringing a new chapter to "The Generational Story Swap," where age was just a number, and laughter was the universal language that connected them all.

The Senior Nature Photographers

In the quiet corner of Whispering Pines Senior Center, a remarkable group known as "The Senior Nature Photographers" embarked on a delightful adventure that combined their love for the great outdoors and a hearty dose of humor.

Every month, this merry band of seasoned photographers set out on a new expedition to capture the beauty of nature through their lenses. Armed with cameras and binoculars, they became a force to be reckoned with, even if their nimbleness was somewhat compromised by the passage of time.

During their first escapade, the group decided to visit a serene lake teeming with graceful swans. Harold, an 80-year-old with a mischievous glint in his eye, set up his tripod at the water's edge. Just as he was about to take a shot, a swan glided gracefully by, but Harold's camera had other plans—it gave a dramatic squawk and promptly plopped into the lake, causing an eruption of laughter.

Not to be outdone, Mildred, an 85-year-old with a knack for finding the unexpected, accidentally captured a squirrel mid-acrobatic leap instead of the intended bird perched on a branch. She proudly proclaimed her photo as the "Squirrel Samba" and insisted it was a rare sighting.

Their next outing took them to a picturesque meadow adorned with colorful wildflowers. Edward, a sprightly 88-

year-old, discovered that his zoom lens was stuck on maximum magnification. Undeterred, he managed to capture an extreme close-up of a ladybug that seemed as big as a basketball, and the resulting photo had the group in fits of laughter.

As the months went by, the Senior Nature Photographers continued their escapades, each one filled with moments of unexpected hilarity. From chasing butterflies with butterfly nets to trying to capture the perfect shot while ducking behind trees, their enthusiasm knew no bounds.

Their photo exhibitions became a highlight of the center's activities, and the seniors' creative captions and anecdotes turned their blunders into endearing tales. The "Squirrel Samba" and "Giant Ladybug" became iconic pieces, reminding everyone that life's imperfections and surprises are what make it truly remarkable.

Through their shared laughter and love for the natural world, the Senior Nature Photographers not only captured beautiful snapshots but also created lasting memories and friendships. Their uplifting and funny stories reminded everyone that age is just a number, and the joy of discovery and camaraderie knows no limits, especially when exploring the wonders of nature together.

The Joyful Sing-Along

At the Sunny Meadows Retirement Home, an enchanting event known as "The Joyful Sing-Along" was a cherished tradition that brought smiles and laughter to the residents. Every Wednesday afternoon, the community room would transform into a lively stage for an unforgettable musical experience.

As the pianist began to play, the seniors gathered with eager anticipation. Martha, the spirited 87-year-old, took her place at the front, ready to lead the singing with her vibrant energy. Her voice might not have been as strong as in her youth, but her enthusiasm was contagious.

The sing-along started with an old classic, "You Are My Sunshine," and soon enough, the room was filled with a harmonious blend of voices. Arthur, a retired mechanic with a deep baritone, belted out the lyrics with a gusto that surprised everyone, and even Martha had to chuckle at his unexpected talent.

As the playlist continued, the seniors' choices ranged from timeless ballads to toe-tapping tunes. The highlight, however, was the impromptu rendition of "Twist and Shout." Martha, fueled by her determination to relive her dancing days, attempted a little twist herself, only to lose her balance and end up in a fit of giggles. The whole room joined in, and soon, the Joyful Sing-Along turned into a full-fledged dance party.

Lenny, the mischievous 92-year-old, stole the show with his unconventional dance moves that he claimed were inspired by his days as a disco king. The residents couldn't contain their laughter as Lenny grooved his way across the room, spreading infectious joy to everyone around him.

Amidst the laughter and merriment, the seniors forged bonds that transcended age. They swapped stories of their favorite songs, shared memories of bygone dance halls, and even brainstormed a plan to create their own music video. The Joyful Sing-Along became more than just a musical event; it became a source of unity and a reminder that age is just a number when it comes to having fun and embracing life.

And so, week after week, the Sunny Meadows Retirement Home resonated with laughter, camaraderie, and the sound of voices lifted in song. The Joyful Sing-Along wasn't just a tradition; it was a celebration of life, love, and the enduring spirit of the seniors who proved that you're never too old to sing, dance, and create moments of pure, unbridled joy.

The Letters to My Younger Self

Every week, a group of residents gathered to write letters filled with advice, anecdotes, and a touch of wit to their younger selves. Clara, a spirited 93-year-old, kicked off the project with a chuckle-worthy tale of her fashion faux pas from the 1950s, when she confidently wore mismatched shoes to a dance and danced the night away, blissfully unaware.

Walter, a retired accountant with a penchant for practical jokes, shared a letter recounting his escapades of cleverly rearranging his boss's office furniture overnight, just to see the confusion unfold the next morning. The room erupted in laughter as he confessed his secret, and even the staff members couldn't help but join in.

The letters were a delightful mix of life lessons and hilarious anecdotes. Lillian, a former schoolteacher, wrote a letter to herself about the time she accidentally mistook a stapler for a toy during a lesson and ended up "stapling" a student's drawing to the wall. Her witty advice to "double-check your classroom supplies" had everyone in stitches.

The project also Inspired unexpected creativity. Arthur, a retired carpenter, attached a tiny wooden replica of a birdhouse to his letter, sharing the tale of the time he accidentally built a birdhouse with a door that was too small for any bird to enter. He affectionately referred to it as the "Avian Airbnb."

As the weeks went by, the collection of letters grew, and the seniors found joy in sharing their stories and wisdom. The project culminated in a heartwarming event where the residents read their letters aloud to each other, their laughter filling the room with a sense of camaraderie and shared experiences.

The "Letters to My Younger Self" became more than just a creative exercise; they became a source of inspiration, humor, and a reminder that life's quirks and mishaps are what make it truly memorable. The project proved that no matter the age, there's always room for laughter, reflection, and the joy of connecting with others through the tales of our past.

About the Author

Charlie Aubrey is a certified nutritionist and a content writer, who is keen on making seniors (elders) have a great and wonderful experience of their livelihood to the fullest.